Writing Stories
Scary Stories

Anita Ganeri

Heinemann
LIBRARY

Chicago, Illinois

Edited by Dan Nunn, Rebecca Rissman,
and Sian Smith
Designed by Joanna Hinton-Malivoire
Original illustrations © Capstone Global Library 2013
Picture research by Ruth Blair
Production by Sophia Argyris
Originated by Capstone Global Library Ltd
Printed in the United States of America in
North Mankato, Minnesota

ISBN: 978 1 4329 7533 3 (Hardback)
ISBN: 978 1 4329 7540 1 (Paperback)

Cataloging-in-Publication Data is available at the
Library of Congress website.
Ganeri, Anita, 1961-
  Scary stories / Anita Ganeri.
    pages cm.—(Writing Stories)
  Includes bibliographical references and index.
  ISBN 978-1-4329-7533-3 (hb)—ISBN 978-1-4329-
7540-1 (pb) 1. Horror tales—Authorship. 2. Creative
writing. I. Title.

  PN3377.5.H67G36 2013
  808.3'8738—dc23   2012043116

Acknowledgments
We would like to thank the following for permission
to reproduce photographs: Alamy p.5 (© tony
french); Getty Images p.7 (© Bettmann); Shutterstock
background images and design features, pp.4
(© SergiyN), 6 (© dragon_fang), 8 (© CREATISTA),
9 (© Kamira), 12 (© Linda Bucklin), 14 (© Devid
Camerlynck), 16 (© Monkey Business Images), 18 (©
Ensuper), 20 (© Monkey Business Images), 22 (©
Estremo), 24 (© Nomad_Soul), 26 (© doglikehorse)

Cover photographs reproduced with permission
of Shutterstock: spooky tree (© Nejron Photo),
background (© prudkov).

Every effort has been made to contact copyright
holders of material reproduced in this book. Any
omissions will be rectified in subsequent printings if
notice is given to the publisher.

All the Internet addresses (URLs) given in this book
were valid at the time of going to press. However,
due to the dynamic nature of the Internet, some
addresses may have changed, or sites may have
changed or ceased to exist since publication. While
the author and publisher regret any inconvenience
this may cause readers, no responsibility for any
such changes can be accepted by either the author
or the publisher.

Some words are shown in bold, **like this**. You can find out what they mean by looking in the glossary.

Contents

Follow this symbol to read a scary story.

What Is a Story?

A story is a piece of **fiction** writing. It tells the reader about made-up people, places, and events. A story needs a **setting, characters**, and a **plot**. You should try to figure these out before you start writing.

There are lots of different types of stories.
You can write mystery stories, funny stories,
fairy tales, adventure stories, animal
stories, and lots more. This book is about
writing scary stories.

Scary Stories

A scary story should have spooky **characters** and a scary **setting**, such as a haunted house or castle. It should be exciting and scary at the same time.

A Christmas Carol by Charles Dickens is a famous scary story. It tells the tale of a very mean man, named Scrooge, who is haunted by the ghosts of Christmas past, present, and future. In the end, Scrooge becomes much kinder and more generous.

Collecting Ideas

You can get ideas for writing your own scary story from books, the Internet, TV, or from your imagination. It is also good to read scary stories by other writers. This can spark ideas and help you make your own writing better.

Quickly write down any ideas you have
in a notebook so that you do not forget
them. Then you can go back to them
later. Keep the notebook handy at all
times, even by your bed. You never know
when an amazing idea will come.

Plot Planning

Before you start writing, you need to plan your **plot**. This means what happens in your story. The plot needs a beginning, a middle, and an end. You can try using a **story mountain** to help you.

Middle
The main action happens. There may be a problem for one of your characters.

Beginning
Set the scene and introduce your main **characters**.

Ending
The problem is solved and the story ends.

 Your story starts at one side of the mountain, goes up to the top, then goes down the other side.

You could also try marking the main events on a **timeline**. This will help you put them in the right order. Here is a timeline for the scary story in this book.

Children on vacation see an old house.

A boy tells them that the house is haunted.

They say that they don't believe in ghosts.

The boy takes them to the house.

Inside the house, they hear spooky noises.

Then they see a ghostly figure.

They run away from the house.

They are sure they know who the ghost is.

Starting Your Story

Your story needs a strong beginning that grabs your readers' attention. It should make them want to keep reading. It is also a good place to introduce your main **characters**.

Sam looked up at the rambling old house on the hill and shivered.

Give your story a scary start.

A Spooky Story

Sam looked up at the rambling old house on the hill and shivered.

Daisy followed his gaze. It was the first day of the children's summer vacation. While their parents were inside unpacking, the twins had gone into the backyard to explore.

Can you think of a different beginning to the story?

Spooky Settings

Setting the scene means deciding on the place and time in which your story is set. It tells your reader where and when the story happens. It brings your story to life. An old, creepy house, like the one below, is a great **setting** for a scary story.

The children couldn't stop looking at the creepy house. It was crumbling and covered in ivy. It had broken windows and a big wooden door. It looked old and gloomy, and it creaked in the wind. Daisy thought that it was the spookiest place she had ever seen.

Describe what your setting looks and sounds like.

Character Building

Create strong and interesting **characters** for your story. Keep fact files, like the ones below, for the main characters. Think about what they look like and about their thoughts and feelings.

Character fact file
Characters: Sam and Daisy (twins)
Age: About 8
Look like: Short, dark hair
Personalities: Curious; very daring
Like: Going on vacation; having adventures
Dislike: Green vegetables; having to go to bed

Character fact file
Character: Mysterious boy
Age: Unknown
Looks like: Small; pale-skinned
Personality: Quiet; sad; faraway look
Likes: Telling stories
Dislikes: Not being believed

The twins and the mysterious boy are the main characters in our story.

Suddenly, a boy appeared next to them. Sam and Daisy jumped.

"It's haunted," the boy said, pointing at the house. "A hundred years ago, a boy who lived there died in a terrible accident. Today, his ghost haunts the house."

There was something strange about the boy, the twins thought. He was very pale, and he looked very sad.

In the Middle

The middle of your story is where the main action happens. You might have several ideas for how your story will work out. Use a **story map**, like the one below, to help you decide which idea will work best.

Boy tells twins house is haunted.

1. Boy leaves twins alone. Twins never see boy again.

2. Boy tells twins he has a key. Boy takes twins into house.

You need to decide which direction your story will go in.

"We don't believe in ghosts," said Sam and Daisy, together.

The boy shrugged. He told the twins that he would prove it. He had a key to the house and could let them in.

"Okay," said Daisy, bravely. "But we'll have to be quick. Our parents will be looking for us."

 Can you think of why the boy might have a key to the house?

Speaking Parts

Dialogue means the words people say. You can use it in your story to bring your **characters** to life and make them more believable. It is also a useful way to bring your readers into the action.

"What's that?" said Sam, as they stood in the dusty hallway. "I'm sure I heard a noise."

Put **quotation marks** around the spoken words.

"What's that?" said Sam, as they stood in the dusty hallway. "I'm sure I heard a noise."

"I heard it, too," said Daisy. "It sounded like someone crying."

The boy said nothing. He just sighed sadly.

"It seems to be getting closer," whispered Sam.

"Yikes!" squeaked Daisy. "It's a..."

Dialogue can make your writing more **dramatic** and exciting.

What Happens Next?

The middle of your story is also where your **characters** face a problem or there is a **dramatic** event. Here are some dramatic events that could happen in your scary story. Can you think of any other ideas?

- The twins see a ghost.
- The boy vanishes.
- The owner of the house appears.
- The twins are trapped inside the house.
- The house falls down.

Several things might happen at the same time.

"...ghost!"

In front of them stood the ghostly figure of a boy. He looked very sad. The twins stood still. They were too frightened to move. They looked around for the boy they had come with. But he was nowhere to be seen.

The middle of your story should keep your readers guessing.

Exciting Writing

In a scary story, it is important to make your writing exciting. Choose your words carefully. For example, add lots of interesting **adjectives** to describe your **characters** and **setting**.

Useful adjectives

creepy

gloomy

hair-raising

terrified

ghostly

Can you think of any others?

Sam and Daisy were terrified. Alone in the creepy house, they trembled with fear. Where had the mysterious boy gone? What was the ghostly shape? They looked at each other. Then they ran out of the house as fast as they could.

Can you pick out the adjectives on this page?

Twist in the Tale

The ending of your story is where you tie up any loose ends for your **characters**. Your ending can be happy or sad, or have a clever or surprising twist. Here are some ideas for endings for the story in this book.

The mysterious boy turns out to be the ghost.

The twins see the ghost again the next day.

The twins' parents see the ghost.

Can you think of another ending?

The twins never went back to the house. And they never saw the mysterious boy again. They spent the rest of their vacation hoping that he would turn up.

But secretly, both Sam and Daisy were certain that the boy and the ghost were the same person.

Use your ending to tell your readers what happens to your characters.

More Top Tips

1 A scary story should be exciting. Use short sentences or phrases to speed up the **pace** of your writing and add excitement.

2 Read your story out loud when you have finished it. This will help you see if it flows well all the way to the end.

3 Read your story through and correct any mistakes. You might need to do this several times before you are happy with it.

4 Do some research for your scary story by visiting a haunted house or castle. Don't forget your notebook for jotting down ideas.

5 Draw pictures of your **characters** and **setting**. This can help you bring them to life and describe what they are like.

6 Don't give too much away early in your story. In a scary story, you want your reader to keep guessing all the way to the end.

Glossary

adjective word that describes nouns (nouns are naming words)

character person in a piece of writing

dialogue words that characters say

dramatic very exciting

fiction piece of writing that is about made-up places, events, and characters

pace speed at which a story moves along

plot what happens in a story

quotation marks marks that show the words someone has spoken

setting time and place in which a story is set

story map diagram that helps you decide the next step of the plot

story mountain mountain-shaped diagram that helps you plan out a story

timeline list of events in the order in which they happen

Find Out More

Books

Ganeri, Anita. *Writing Stories*. Chicago: Raintree, 2013.

Stowell, Louie, and Jane Chisholm. *Write Your Own Story Book*. Tulsa, Okla.: EDC, 2011.

Warren, Celia. *How to Write Stories* (How to Write). Laguna Hills, Calif.: QEB, 2007.

Writing Stories
Scary Stories

- How can I get ideas for a scary story?
- When should I introduce my main characters?
- How can I use dialogue to bring my characters to life?

Read this book to learn the answers to all these questions and more!

This book teaches readers how to write scary stories. Key features of the genre are explained, top tips are given, and readers are guided through the process of writing their own story. Engaging photographs, eye-catching illustrations, and a wealth of ideas bring the genre to life. A spooky story running throughout the book draws readers in, offers concrete examples of how the tips can be put into practice, and will inspire readers to start writing their own scary stories.

Books in the **Writing Stories** series:
Adventure Stories
Animal Stories
Fairy Tales
Funny Stories
Mystery Stories
Scary Stories

Language Arts • Level N

Heinemann
Raintree

a capstone imprint   www.capstonepub.com

Heinemann
firSt
Library

ISBN 978-1-4329-7540-1

90000

9 781432 975401

Writing Stories
Funny Stories